P9-ELX-591

Brooks Library Media Center.
2700 Stonebridge Blvd.
Aurora, IL 60504

Brooks Library Media Center
2700 Stonebridge Blvd.
Aurora, IL 60504

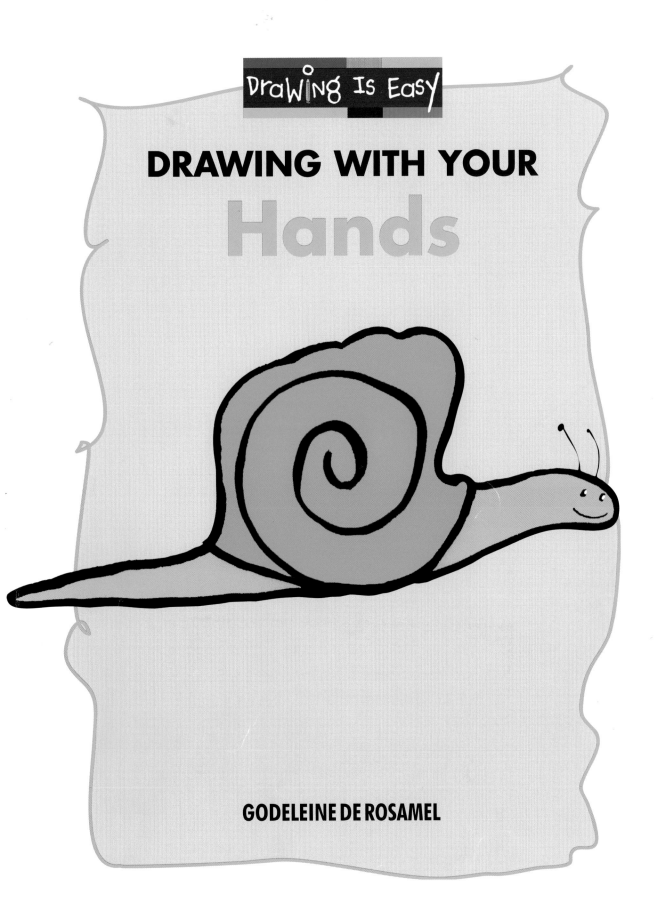

DRAWING WITH YOUR
Hands

GODELEINE DE ROSAMEL

Gareth Stevens Publishing
A WORLD ALMANAC EDUCATION GROUP COMPANY

Please visit our web site at: www.garethstevens.com
For a free color catalog describing Gareth Stevens Publishing's list
of high-quality books and multimedia programs, call 1-800-542-2595 (USA) or
1-800-387-3178 (Canada). Gareth Stevens Publishing's fax: (414) 332-3567.

Library of Congress Cataloging-in-Publication Data

De Rosamel, Godeleine.
　　[Dessine avec tes mains. English]
　　Drawing with your hands/by Godeleine De Rosamel.
　　　　p. cm. — (Drawing is easy)
　　Summary: Step-by-step illustrations demonstrate how to use outlines of hands as
the starting point for drawings.
　　Includes bibliographical references.
　　ISBN 0-8368-3629-4 (lib. bdg.)
　　1. Drawing—Technique—Juvenile literature.　2. Hand in art—Juvenile literature.
[1. Drawing—Technique.]　I. Title.
NC655.R6713　2003
741.2—dc21　　　　　　　　　　　　　　　　　　　2002036535

This edition first published in 2003 by
Gareth Stevens Publishing
A World Almanac Education Group Company
330 West Olive Street, Suite 100
Milwaukee, WI　53212　USA

This edition © 2003 by Gareth Stevens, Inc.
First published as *Dessine: Avec tes mains* in 2000 by Editions Casterman.
© 2000 by Casterman.　Additional end matter © 2003 by Gareth Stevens, Inc.

Translation:　Patrice Lantier
Gareth Stevens editor:　Dorothy L. Gibbs
Gareth Stevens designer:　Melissa Valuch
Cover design:　Melissa Valuch

All rights reserved.　No part of this book may be reproduced, stored in a retrieval system,
or transmitted in any form or by any means, electronic, mechanical, photocopying, recording,
or otherwise, without the prior written permission of the copyright holder.

Printed in the United States of America

1 2 3 4 5 6 7 8 9 07 06 05 04 03

Table of Contents

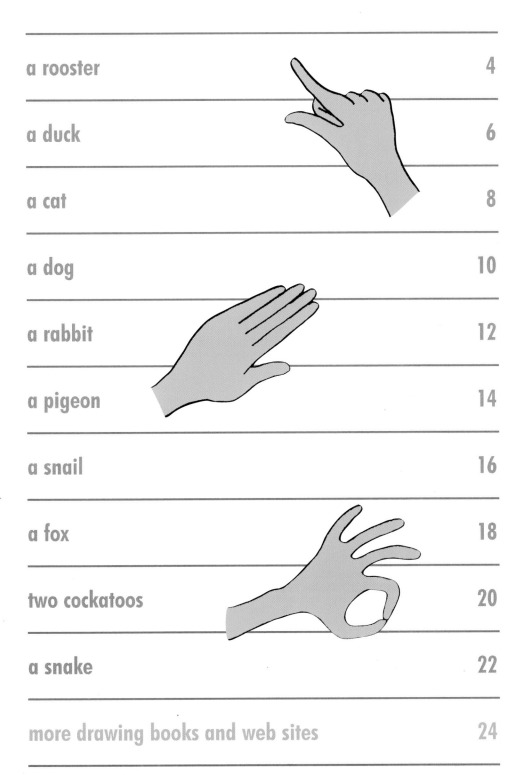

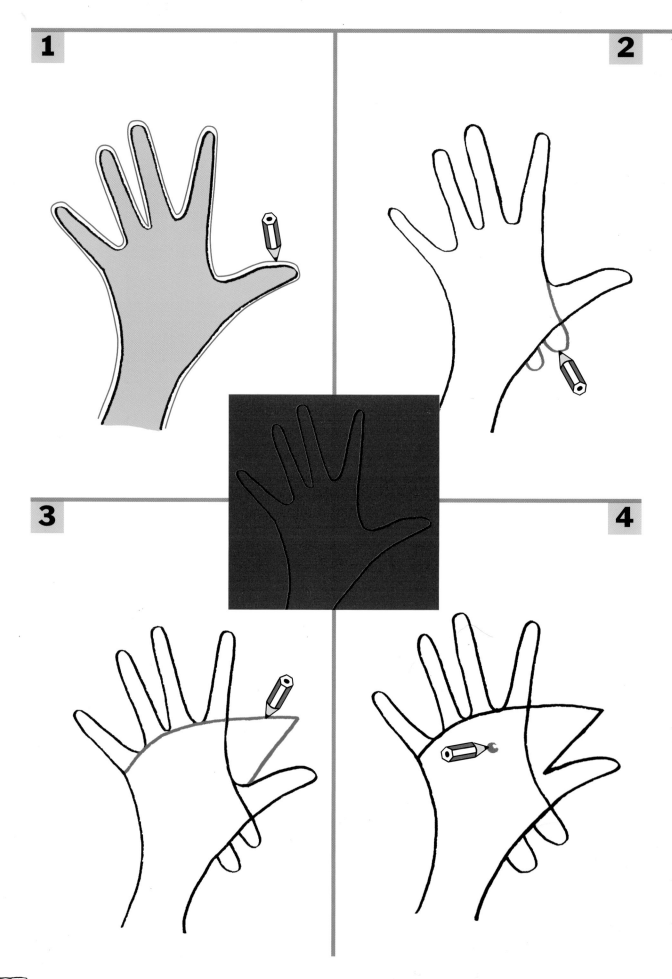

a rooster

COCK-A-DOODLE-DOO

a hen

a young rooster

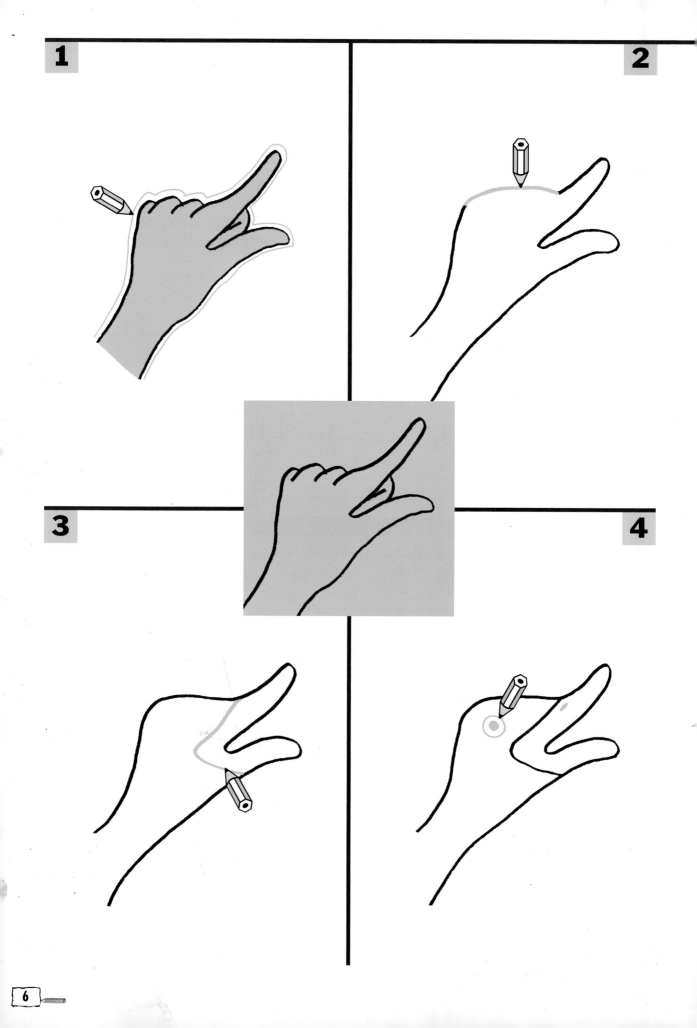

a duck

an angry duck   a friendly duck   a goose

1

2

3

4

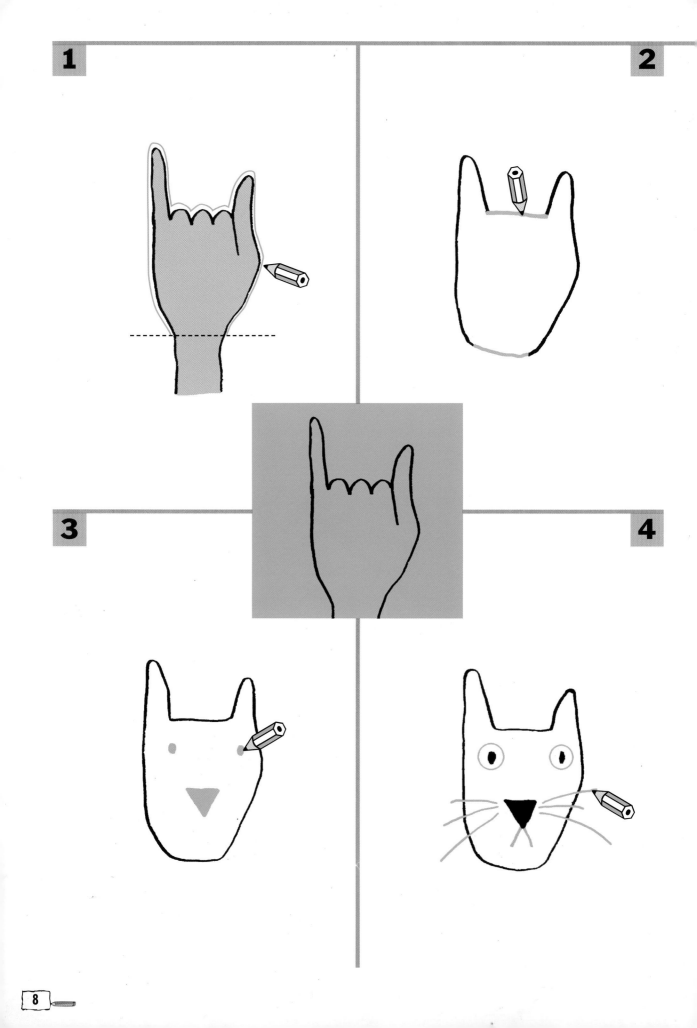

a cat

an owl

a pig

1

2

3

4

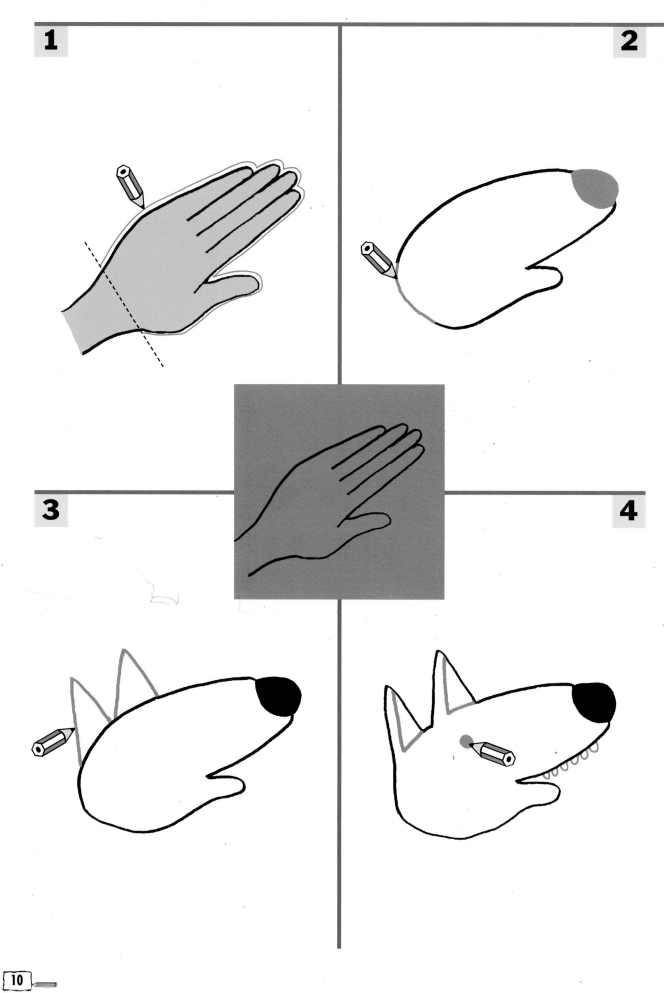

a dog

a dog with long ears

a bear

a rabbit

a fish

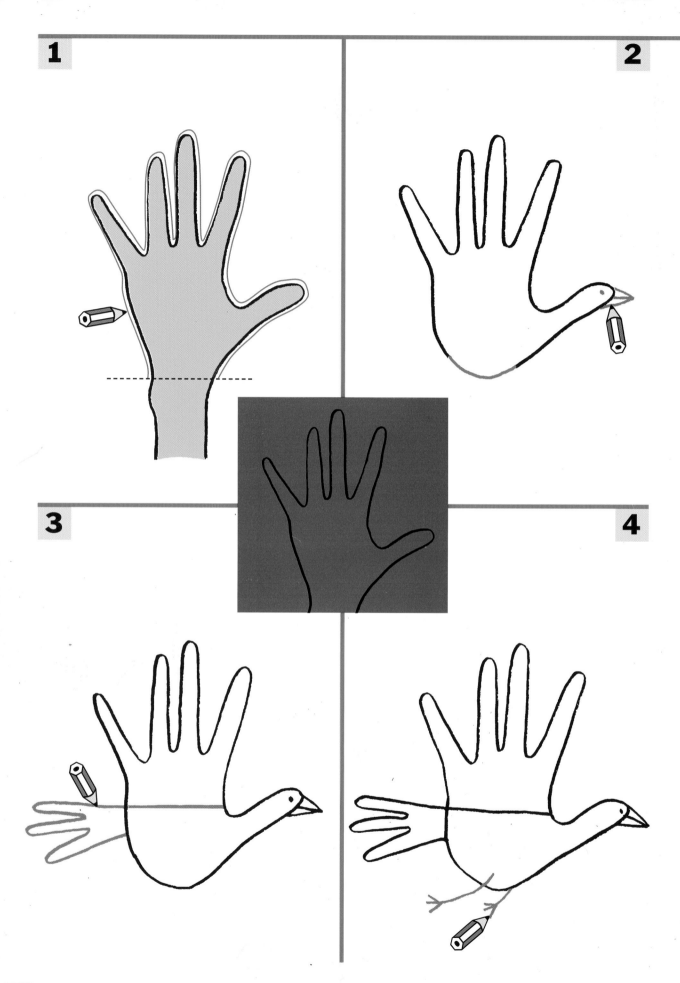

a pigeon

a pigeon in a puddle | a pigeon walking | a duck

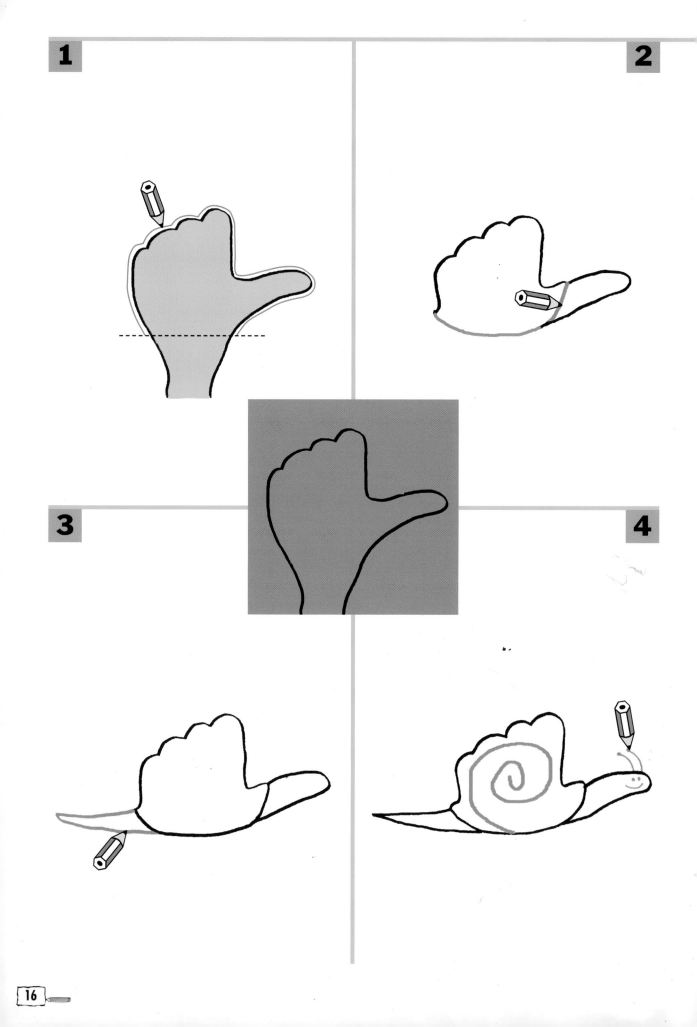

1

2

3

4

a snail

a chicken   **a turtle**   **a camel**

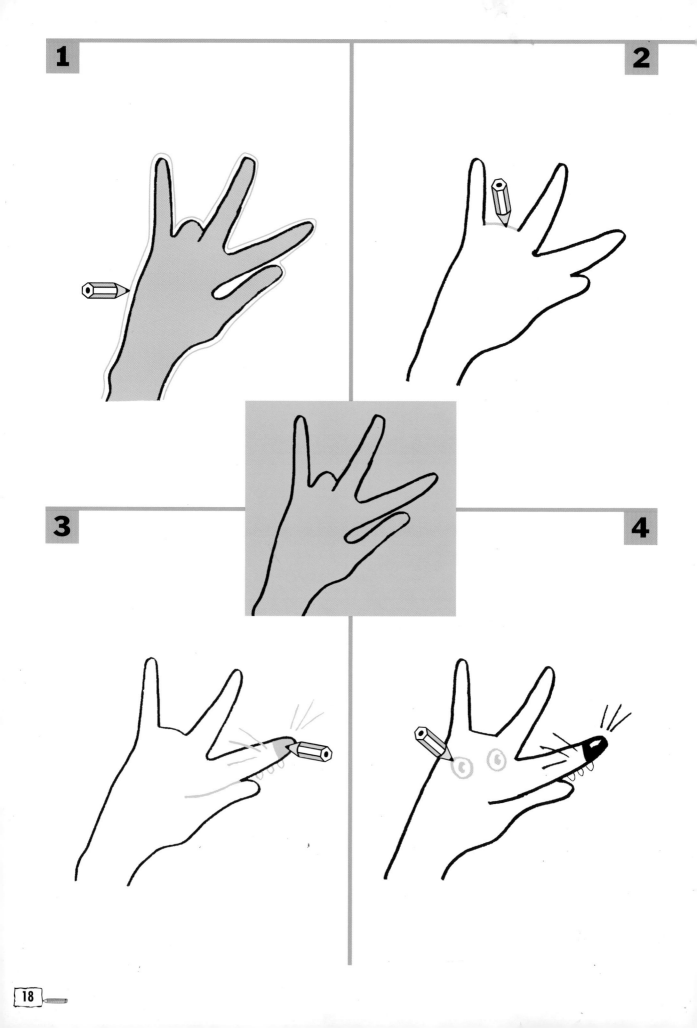

a fox

a hungry fox

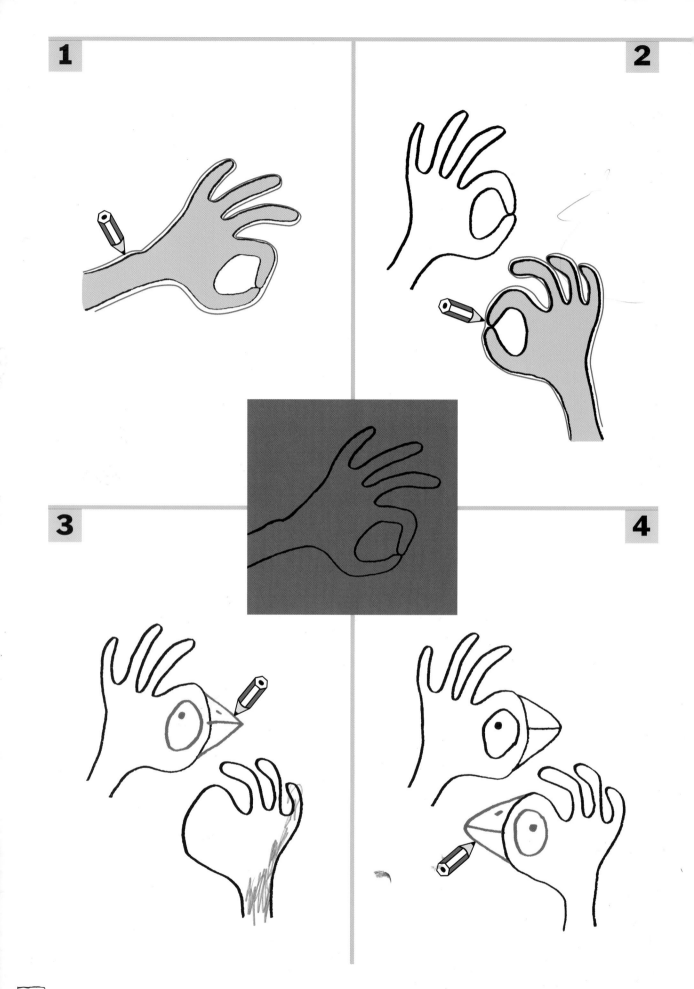

two cockatoos

a bird flying

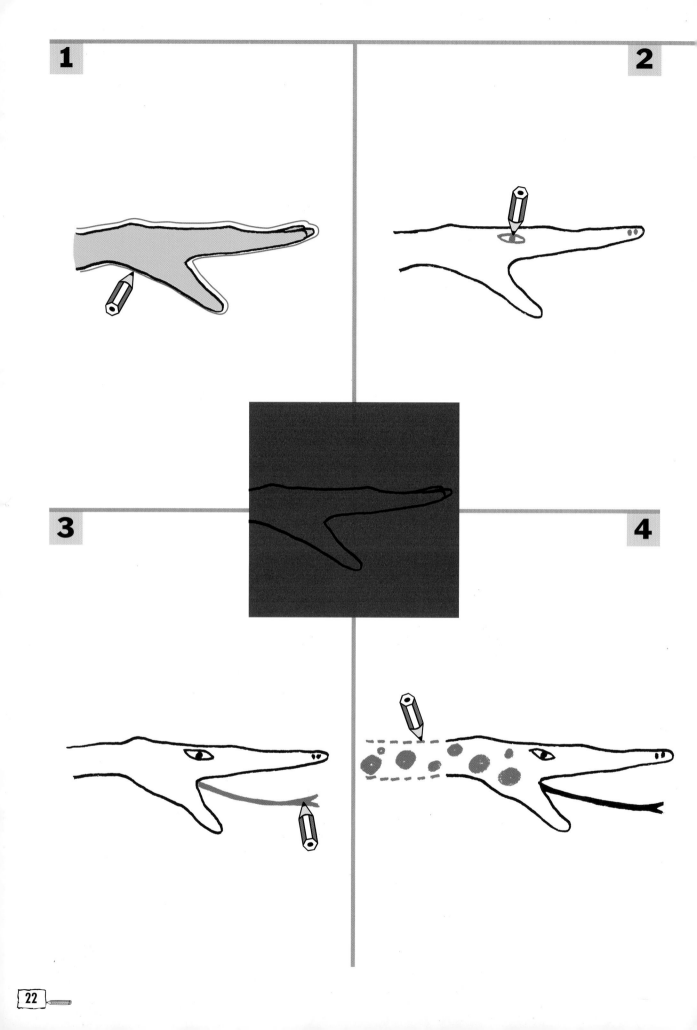

a crocodile

more drawing books

- *Hand-Shaped Art*
  Diane Bonica
  (McGraw-Hill)

- *Hands Up Art Activities*
  Pam Campbell
  (Teaching & Learning Company)

- *I Can Draw Country Animals. I Can Draw Animals* (series)
  Hélène Leroux-Hugon
  (Gareth Stevens)

web sites

- EnchantedLearning.com's Handprint Crafts
  www.zoomdinosaurs.com/crafts/handprint/

- Learn to Draw: A Project 4 Kids
  www.billybear4kids.com/Learn2Draw/Learn2Draw.html